igloobooks

# CONTENTS

# INTRODUCTION

Join in the craze of the century and learn how to perform incredible tricks with your fidget spinner!

This book is packed with 50 amazing fidget spinner tricks ranging from basic techniques all the way to awesome show-stoppers. Plus, with the handy step-by-step guides for every trick, and helpful photos, too, you'll be a fidget spinner expert in no time!

# FIDGET SPINNERS EXPLAINED

Fidget spinners come in all sorts of different shapes, designs and even colours. In fact, some of the tricks shown later on work best when using different coloured spinners. Before you get started, take a look below to get to know what each part of your fantastic fidget spinner does.

## BLADES

The rotating parts of the spinner. Make sure nothing is touching the blades so they can move freely.

## BLADE WEIGHTS

The weights ensure smooth rotation of the spinner.

## RAISED CAPS

These allow you to hold the spinner at the top and the bottom, so the blades can rotate freely.

# EASY TRICKS

## STEP 1

The very first thing you need to master! Hold the spinner in your right hand (left if you're left handed) by placing your forefinger on the spinner's top cap and your thumb underneath its bottom cap.

## STEP 2

Use the forefinger on your other hand to give one of the blades a quick flick, causing the spinner to rotate.

# ONE HAND FLICK ❷

## STEP 1

A skill you need to master for tricks where you hold a spinner in each hand. As before, hold the spinner in one hand by placing your forefinger on the top cap and your thumb underneath its bottom cap.

## STEP 2

This time, flick one of the blades by using a finger on the same hand. Experiment to see if the best results come from using your middle, third or little finger.

# BALANCING SPIN  ③

## STEP 1

Start the spinner rotating in the usual way by holding it between forefinger and thumb and giving it a good flick with a finger on your other hand.

## STEP 2

When the spinner is rotating smoothly, gently lift your forefinger from the top cap. The spinner should now be nicely balanced and rotating on your thumb!

# DOUBLE SPIN

## STEP 1

Hold the first spinner between the forefinger and thumb of your left hand and give it a good smooth flick with a finger on your right hand to set it rotating.

## STEP 2

Place the second spinner between the forefinger and thumb of your right hand. Then start rotating this spinner too, with the flick of a finger on your right hand. Now carefully lift each forefinger!

## STEP 1

Stack two spinners between your forefinger and thumb, holding firmly on the top cap of the first spinner and the bottom cap of the second spinner.

## STEP 2

First flick the bottom spinner to set it in motion. Now carefully flick the top spinner as well, making sure nothing is in the way to stop the rotation of the bottom spinner.

You might find it easier to flick both spinners together rather than one at a time. To do this, you must make sure that the blades of each spinner are perfectly lined up together before flicking them.

# TABLE STACK

Stack the spinners on a flat surface, keeping the stack in place by pressing your finger on the top spinner's cap. Make sure all the blades are aligned and then give the blades a firm, smooth flick.

# TABLE STACK 2

## STEP 1

As in **Table Stack** (p.11), stack the spinners and press down on the top cap. But this time, do not align all the blades. This is so they can be flicked separately.

## STEP 2

Starting at the bottom of the stack, flick the bottom blade in a clockwise direction, the middle blade in an anti-clockwise direction, and the top blade in a clockwise direction.

# ELBOW SPIN

Bend your right arm and raise your elbow until it is perfectly horizontal. Place a spinner on your elbow and press down on the top cap with your left forefinger. Flick the blade with your thumb. Now try it with two spinners!

# KNEE SPIN ⑨

Rotate the spinner on your knee. You can do this either sitting up with your knees in front of you or (a bit harder) lying on your back with your knees bent. Now try to keep a spinner revolving on each knee at the same time.

# THUMBS-UP SPIN

## STEP 1

Some more on-the-body spins! Bend the top joint of your thumb upwards, making it as vertical as possible. Place the spinner on top of your thumb and keep in place with your forefinger.

## STEP 2

Flick one of the spinner's blades so it is smoothly rotating, and then lift your forefinger, holding the spinner well out of the way. Now, very carefully straighten your thumb upwards until it is fully vertical.

# KNUCKLE SPIN

Make one of your hands into a fist. Hold the spinner on top of your forefinger knuckle with the forefinger of your other hand. Use the thumb of that other hand to set the spinner in motion and then carefully lift your forefinger.

# BIG TOE SPIN

With your big toe as vertical as possible, place the spinner carefully on the tip. Use a finger to hold the spinner in place until you've got it nicely rotating and balanced, then carefully lift your finger.

# MAGIC SPINNER

## STEP 1

This one's a bit of a cheat, but an absolute show-stopper! Secretly put a small piece of double-sided sticky tape on the spinner's top cap. Then hold the spinner between your forefinger and thumb, ready for your show.

## STEP 2

Flick the spinner to set it in motion. Normally, you would now lift your forefinger from the top but this time you lower your thumb from the bottom.To everyone's amazement, the revolving spinner seems to be flying in the air!

# 2X MAGIC SPINNER 🕙

This trick is very similar to **Magic Spinner** (p.16) only instead of using one spinner, you double the magic by using two! As before, place double-sided sticky tape on the top caps of both spinners. Holding one of the spinners in your left hand, and the other in your right, start both spinners rotating. Then, remove both of your thumbs to see both spinners floating in the air!

## STEP 1

Try this game of chance! Place a die on a firm surface and a spinner on top of the die. Press a finger on the top cap of the spinner and give one of the blades a firm, smooth flick. Carefully lift your finger.

## STEP 2

If you would like to make this trick more challenging, place a stack of spinners on top of the die.

# BOTTLE TOP SPIN 16

Place the spinner on the cap of a plastic bottle and hold with your left forefinger. Flick one of the blades firmly and smoothly with your right forefinger, then lift your left forefinger. If you find this too easy, try a stack of spinners.

# PENCIL TOP SPIN 17

Make sure you use a pencil with a flat top. Use your forefinger to press a spinner to the end of a pencil. Start spinning, then lift your forefinger. This trick is easier if you keep the pointed end of the pencil pressed against a firm surface.

# PAIR OF SPINNERS 18

## STEP 1

Grip the first spinner between the forefinger and thumb of your left hand. Grip the second spinner between the forefinger and thumb of your right hand.

## STEP 2

Remind yourself of the **One Hand Flick** (p.7), where you learned how to rotate a spinner using a finger on the same hand that gripped it. Do this for both spinners.

# SKILLED TRICKS

# HAND PASS

**DIFFICULTY** 🌀🌀🌀

## STEP 1

Hold a spinner vertically between the forefinger and thumb of your left hand. Start to rotate with a good, smooth flick.

## STEP 2

While the spinner is still rotating, 'jump' it across to the forefinger and thumb of your right hand. Make sure your fingers catch the spinner right in the centre, avoiding the blades.

## TOP TIP

For your first few goes, try 'jumping' the spinner across just a few centimetres to perfect your technique. Then gradually move your hands further apart.

# AIR JUMP

**20**

As with the **Hand Pass** (p.22), you again 'jump' the spinner from one hand to the other but this time your first hand tosses it upwards slightly into the air. Again, it's essential that you catch the spinner in the exact centre to keep it rotating.

# SAME HAND JUMP **21**

Rotate the spinner vertically between the forefinger and thumb of your right hand. Toss it slightly into the air and catch it between the forefinger and thumb of the same hand. Remember to catch it in the exact centre to avoid the blades.

# FRIEND PASS

DIFFICULTY

## STEP 1

Have a friend stand near and opposite you, ready with their forefinger and thumb wide apart.

## STEP 2

Rotate the spinner vertically between your forefinger and thumb and then 'jump' it carefully to your friend's wide-open forefinger and thumb. Your throw needs to be as accurate as possible.

## TOP TIP

This trick requires perfect timing from both of you. Try switching around, so your friend is the thrower and you're the receiver.

Your friend's forefinger and thumb need to catch the spinner exactly in the centre, avoiding the blades. This means the spinner should have continued rotating all the way from your hand to theirs.

# HORIZONTAL PASS 23

**DIFFICULTY**

Hold the spinner horizontally between your forefinger and thumb, while your friend also holds their forefinger and thumb horizontally, and as wide open as possible. As before, 'jump' the spinner to your friend's fingers. They must try to catch it by its exact centre, avoiding the blades.

# FOREARM CATCH

**DIFFICULTY**

## STEP 1

Rotate the spinner vertically between the forefinger and thumb of your left hand. Hold your right arm in front of you, with your elbow half bent, so that your forearm is at an angle.

## STEP 2

Pass the spinner under your right forearm and toss it upwards. Catch the spinner, still vertical and spinning, in your right hand.

## TOP TIP

With catching tricks, it helps to bend your knees slightly as you catch.

# OVER LEG JUMP (25)

Sit on a chair with your right heel resting on another chair so your leg is outstretched. Rotate the spinner, then hold it vertically below the right side of your leg, toss it over your leg and catch with your other hand waiting for it below the left side of your leg.

# OVER LEG JUMP 2 (26)

As with **Over Leg Jump** (p.27), carefully toss the spinner over your leg from below its right side. Now, quickly pass that throwing hand under your leg to catch the spinner, still rotating, below your leg's left side.

# DROP CATCH

**DIFFICULTY**

## STEP 1

Hold your left hand a little above your right hand. Grasp the spinner between the forefinger and thumb of your left hand and flick it to give it a smooth rotation.

## STEP 2

Release the spinner from your left hand so that it drops down towards your right hand, waiting a little below it.

As the dropped spinner approaches your right hand, catch it carefully by the central caps so you avoid the blades. This will keep the spinner rotating after it has been caught.

# LIFT CATCH

**28**

**DIFFICULTY**

This is **Drop Catch** (p.28-9) in reverse. Hold the spinner in your right hand and give it a good, smooth flick with the forefinger of your left hand. Now raise your left hand a little above your right hand and toss the spinner up towards it. Catch neatly by the spinner's two central caps.

# KNEE BOUNCE

**DIFFICULTY**

## STEP 1

Hold the spinner horizontally between the forefinger and thumb of your right hand. Flick with another finger on that hand or, if you find it easier, the forefinger of your left hand.

## STEP 2

Raise your right knee slightly and let the spinner fall horizontally on to it. As it falls, flick your knee upwards so that the spinner bounces up towards your hand, which catches it neatly by the two central caps.

# 2X KNEE BOUNCE

 30

## STEP 1

You can do a **2x Knee Bounce** in two ways. First, drop the spinner on to your knee and bounce it twice before flicking it up to catch.

## STEP 2

Second, bounce the spinner from your knee up to your hand once. Then, with it still neatly spinning, drop it on to your knee again and bounce back to your hand a second time.

**TOP TIP**

Remember, don't try to do skilled tricks too quickly. A smooth, controlled technique usually produces better results.

# HAND TWIST

**DIFFICULTY**

## STEP 1

Hold the spinner horizontally, with your forefinger on the central cap at the top and your thumb on the cap at the bottom. Flick the spinner firmly to give it a fast, smooth spin.

## STEP 2

Lifting your forefinger right out of the way, use your thumb to toss the spinner upwards. As the spinner comes back down again, quickly turn your hand over so that you catch it with your thumb now at the top of the spinner and your forefinger at the bottom.

# OVER-THE-ARM

**DIFFICULTY**

## STEP 1

Rotate the spinner horizontally between the forefinger and thumb of your right hand.

## STEP 2

Holding your left forearm stationary above it, toss the spinner upwards so that it loops over your forearm and comes down on the other side for you to catch it.

**TOP TIP** Some people find this trick easier if the spinner is tossed and caught vertically instead. Practise to see which works best for you.

# AROUND THE LEG  DIFFICULTY

## STEP 1

Hold the spinner horizontally in your left hand, raise your left knee and pass the spinner under the knee before releasing it upwards.

## STEP 2

Catch the spinner neatly in your right hand, careful to avoid the blades, so you can keep it rotating.

## TOP TIP

When throwing with one hand and catching with the other, use your strongest hand to do the catching.

# AROUND AGAIN

As with **Around the Leg** (p.34), but when you catch the spinner in your right hand, raise your right leg so you can now immediately go in the other direction. Pass the spinner under your right knee, release it upwards and this time catch it in your left hand.

# COMBO AROUND LEG **35**

A 'combo' is when you follow one spinner trick immediately with another. After completing an **Around the Leg** (p.34), do a **Hand Pass** (p.22) so that you return the spinner to the hand that it started from.

# BACKHAND BOUNCE 36

## STEP 1

Rotate the spinner as fast as you can. Toss it slightly into the air and let it land on the back of the fingers of one hand. Immediately bounce the spinner upwards again so that it crosses to the back of the fingers of the other hand.

## STEP 2

Keep quickly bouncing the spinner from the back of one hand across to the other, before flicking the spinner right up and neatly catching.

## TOP TIP

For this trick to work well, the back of your fingers need to be held as flat as possible.

# EXPERT TRICKS

**DIFFICULTY**

## STEP 1

Hold your hand horizontally, with your thumb at the top. Grip the spinner between thumb and forefinger and start it rotating. Lift your thumb to leave the spinner nicely balanced on the tip of your forefinger.

## STEP 2

Gently flick the spinner upwards a little, and catch it on your middle finger. Then flick it again and catch it on your third finger, then little finger.

## TOP TIP

Practise for this trick by making the spinner jump from your forefinger to middle finger. Then, move on to the other fingers. When you have mastered each separate jump, you're ready to perform the trick!

# 2X FINGER JUMP  38

## STEP 1

As before, hold the spinner between your thumb and forefinger, then lift your thumb to leave the spinner nicely balanced. Repeatedly hop the spinner gently upwards a little so it jumps from one finger to the next.

## STEP 2

When the spinner has reached your little finger, gently flick it upwards, catching it on the tip of your forefinger. Then, make it jump again from one finger to another down to your little finger, finishing with a jump back to your forefinger.

# FINGER TWIST

**DIFFICULTY**

## STEP 1

With the palm of your hand facing upwards, bend your forefinger and balance the spinner on top. Keep it stable with your thumb on the upper cap until the spinner is rotating nicely.

## STEP 2

Twisting your wrist backwards and forwards, move your finger in all sorts of directions – sometimes bent, sometimes half bent – while keeping the spinner constantly balanced and rotating.

# BACKHAND JUMP 40

With your palm facing upwards, place the spinner on your forefinger and rotate. Gently toss the spinner a little into the air. At the same time, quickly turn your hand and bend your forefinger so that you catch the spinner on its second joint.

# BACKHAND JUMP 2 41

DIFFICULTY
ususus

Proceed as above until the spinner is rotating on the second joint of your bent forefinger. Gently toss the spinner a little into the air, at the same time quickly turning your hand so you can catch the spinner on the tip of your middle finger.

# SPINNER SWAP

**DIFFICULTY**

## STEP 1

Hold the first spinner horizontally between your left hand's forefinger and thumb and the second spinner horizontally between your right hand's forefinger and thumb.

## STEP 2

Set each spinner in motion. You do this either by using a finger on the same hand, or a free finger from the other hand. Choose the technique that gives you the fastest rotation for each spinner.

## TOP TIP

So the spinners don't collide during the swap over, make sure you arc one of the spinners clear over the top of the other one.

With your hands at the same level and about 20 cm (8 in) apart, gently toss each spinner to the other hand at the same time, and catch with the spinners still rotating.

# AROUND THE BACK 43 DIFFICULTY

Hold the spinner vertically between the forefinger and thumb of your left hand. Give the spinner a fast rotation, then toss it upwards behind your back so it passes over your right shoulder. Catch the spinner, still rotating, in between the forefinger and thumb of your right hand.

# JUGGLE SPIN

**DIFFICULTY**

## STEP 1

Rotate the spinner horizontally in your left hand. Start with **Around the Back** (p.43), tossing the spinner behind and around your back and catching it, still rotating, in your hand.

## STEP 2

Immediately follow up with an **Around the Leg** (p.34), then a **Knee Bounce** (p.30) on your right knee and one on your left. Finally, catch the spinner between your forefinger and thumb, with it still rotating smoothly.

## TOP TIP

For long or combo tricks, you need to have the spinner rotating as fast as possible, or it will never last until the end!

# SUPER JUGGLE SPIN (45)

Rotate the spinner between forefinger and thumb, toss it into the air and balance it, still rotating fast, on the tip of an upright finger. After an **Around the Leg** (p.34), catch and balance the spinner on your fingertip, and again after a **Knee Bounce** (p.30).

# FINGERTIP PASS (46)

Rotate the spinner horizontally between forefinger and thumb of your right hand. Toss the spinner across to your left hand but catch it by balancing on a fingertip. Toss the spinner back to your right hand, but again, catch it on a fingertip.

# DROP-AND-LIFT

**DIFFICULTY**

## STEP 1

Hold the spinner horizontally between forefinger and thumb and flick to rotate. Drop the spinner a little, at the same time twisting your hand so you can catch it balanced on a fingertip.

## STEP 2

Now toss the spinner upwards from your fingertip, turning your hand so you can grasp it between forefinger and thumb again. Switching from hand to hand between drops and lifts makes this trick even more awesome!

# BLADE-HOLD SPIN 48

Hold the spinner vertically with your forefinger and thumb pinching the middle of one of its blades. Flick the spinner upwards to set it rotating and catch neatly by the central caps – or balanced on a fingertip if you really want to show off!

# SUPER SPIN 49

DIFFICULTY

Balance the rotating spinner on your right forefinger and toss it high into the air so that it's well above your head. Before the spinner comes down again, quickly spin round yourself in a full circle and catch the spinner with the same finger.

# SUPER JUMP

**50**

## STEP 1

Hold the spinner horizontally between your forefinger and thumb and start it rotating. Pull your forefinger out of the way and toss the spinner slightly into the air, at the same time raising your hand vertically so you can catch the spinner on the very top of your forefinger.

## STEP 2

When you're sure you have the spinner nicely balanced, toss it gently across to the top of the next finger. Continue right down to the top of your little finger.

## TOP TIP

A difficult trick like this requires amazing precision so relax and don't rush. This is the secret behind all the expert spinner tricks.